The CHRISTMAS TREE BOOK
A Collection of Fantasy Trees

General Publishing Group
Los Angeles

Publisher: W. Quay Hays
Editorial Director: Peter L. Hoffman
Editor: Dana A. Stibor
Designer: Judy Glenzer
Production Director: Trudihope Schlomowitz
Prepress Manager: Bill Castillo
Production Artists: Thomas Hultgren and Bill Neary
Production Assistants: Tom Archibeque, David Chadderdon, Russel Lockwood, Gaston Moraga, and Robert Penczar
Editorial Assistant: Dominic Friesen

For information:

General Publishing Group, Inc.
2701 Ocean Park Boulevard, Suite 140
Santa Monica, CA 90405

Library of Congress Cataloging-in-Publication Data

Hays, Sharon.
    The Christmas tree book : a collection of fantasy trees /
compiled by Sharon Hays.
        p.   cm.
    ISBN 1-57544-106-3 (hc.)
    1. Christmas trees—Pictorial works.   I. Title.
GT4989.H39   1998
394.2663—dc21
                                                                                        98-38141
                                                                                        CIP

Printed in the USA by Worzalla
10 9 8 7 6 5 4 3 2 1

General Publishing Group
Los Angeles

For Paris, Mason, and Piper,
who keep the joy of Christmas
flourishing in my home.

Introduction

*E*ach December, when the days become shorter and the evening air begins to bite with the first frost, the anticipation of Christmas fills the home. Children suddenly start to behave better, shopping becomes more purposeful, and dusty attics and overflowing garages are descended upon to unearth stacks of brittle boxes and bulging trunks containing carefully wrapped Christmas decorations.

Mantles are cleared, centerpieces put away, and window boxes stripped of the last remnants of fall. The baskets of dried orange and red maple leaves and the colorful Indian corn and harvest orbs have lost their favored place at the table. The festive Christmas decorating begins!

Without a doubt, the single most important decorating decision leading up to Christmas is choosing the tree. Barren lots all over town have miraculously sprouted forests of evergreens, and the scent of pine wafts through the night air, beckoning you to walk among their majesty. The family piles into the car and sets off to choose the lucky tree that will grace the living room, den, entranceway, or dining room of the home.

Strolling through the Christmas tree lot you come across trees of all shapes and sizes. A magnificent Grand Douglas fir stands 15-feet tall with wide outstretched branches dripping with sap. Nearby is a modest six-foot Blue Spruce evoking images of an English Victorian Christmas, its needles soft and velvety. Which will it be? How can a family possibly decide? Each tree is individual in character and style and everyone has an opinion to express about this lovely conifer. One must walk slowly around and around the tree, observing it from all angles, careful not to miss the flaws and imperfections that will surely glare at you once you've brought it home.

Thank goodness for the ornaments, for they are the icing on the cake. Their job is to distract the eye from any irregularities and magically transform this once plain, simple arbor into a Cinderella. A feast for the eyes. A creation too beautiful to ignore. This is the essence of *The Christmas Tree Book*.

It is hoped that the images in *The Christmas Tree Book* will evoke fond memories of Christmases past and recall special family outings to those magical places where the magnificent Christmas tree stood tall and regal—in the town square, neighborhood church, glorious hotel lobby, or stately museum, a noble symbol of peace and joy—and, finally, inspire you to celebrate your or your family's own individual character and style. Instead of dragging out the same tired old ornaments, surprise yourself and your family and create a work of art! After all, Christmas only comes 'round once a year!

Noël
Sharon Hays

Foreword

The Christmas tree is the universally recognized symbol of Christmas. Many ancient myths and legends revolve around the evergreen. One such legend holds that in Roman times fir trees were decorated with baubles and trinkets to celebrate the sun gods, for they compared the sun to the spreading branches of the great trees. It is thought that our own Christmas tree decorations reflect this tradition—the lights representing lightning; the decorations the sun, the moon, and the stars; and the animal ornaments portraying the pagan sacrifice to the sun god.

Better known is the legend of the Christmas tree in Germany. It is said that a poor forester brought a freezing orphaned child into his home one wintry Christmas Eve, fed and clothed him, and gave him a warm bed to sleep in. The next morning the forester and his family awoke to the heavenly song of angels, and the small house was filled with gifts and food spread upon the family dining table. The lost child was the Christ Child, and as he left he broke a branch from a fir tree and put it in the earth and told the forester that whenever the branch bore fruit, it would bring the man good fortune and remind him of Christ's birthday.

The first written record of a Christmas tree appearing in popular culture is from a citizen of Strassburg, Germany, who, in 1605, observed that fir trees were decorated with colored papers, fruits, and candies in the fashionable parlors of the city. Despite the initial disapproval of the church, the Christmas tree began to flourish in both Protestant and Catholic homes and shortly thereafter it began to appear inside the churches. Germany is now firmly established as the "home" of traditional

Christmas with local *Christkindlmarkts* appearing in nearly every German town. These markets are often located in town squares and sell beautiful handmade ornaments, toys, and decorations. The largest of the markets are in Munich and Nuremberg.

It would take many years for the Christmas tree to catch on outside the courts and royal

Scene of a traditional German Christkindlmarkt.

residences of the European nobility, but by the late 17th century the tradition spread across the continent and into England. The Christmas tree became well established in North America with the first recorded sale of trees taking place in New York City in 1851. It is widely believed that in 1856, during President Franklin Pierce's administration, the first decorated Christmas tree appeared in the White House, although there is no documentation to support this. The more commonly held belief is that the first tree was actually on display during Benjamin Harrison's administration, spanning from 1889 to 1893. The first "National Christmas Tree" was erected on the grounds of the White House in 1923 during Calvin Coolidge's term in office. Every year since, a president or vice president has lit the tree, which is now a living tree planted in Sherman Square, southeast of the White House.

Undated woodcut portraying a Victorian Christmas at Windsor Castle, England, in the late 19th century. (L-R) Duchess of Kent, Queen Victoria, and Prince Albert with children.

The nation's only living National Shrine is the General Grant Tree, a giant sequoia that stands 268.1 feet tall and is located in wondrous Sequoia and Kings Canyon National Park in California. Named the Nation's Christmas Tree in 1926 by President Coolidge, the tree is also a living memorial to the men and women of the United States who have given their lives in service to their country. Each year, during the Christmas season, park rangers place a large wreath at the base of the Grant Tree, remembering those valiant soldiers.

Today, the Christmas tree is the centerpiece of the home during the holidays, and more than 33 million trees are harvested annually in North America alone. Christmas trees are being decorated by celebrities and auctioned off at fundraisers—many of which appear in this book—and hospital auxiliary clubs have also jumped on the decorating bandwagon, raising thousands of dollars for local charities. Hotels, places of worship, trendy eateries, and government buildings all erect Christmas trees and spend top dollar to have them professionally decorated and displayed.

Scott, Zelda, and Scottie Fitzgerald doing the kick step in front of their Christmas tree in the 1920s.

Whether natural or artificial, 50 feet tall or tabletop high, the Christmas tree has established itself as a family tradition in most Christian homes and as one of the holiday's most cherished symbols.

Rockefeller Center

The celebration of Christmas in Rockefeller Center started informally in 1931 when a small tree was placed on a construction site for the workmen to enjoy while collecting their pay on Christmas Eve. The first formal tree was erected in 1933 on the sidewalk in front of the RCA Building. Originally, the tree was untrimmed, except for a lighted star on its top, and was illuminated by floodlights each evening after dusk. Today, more than 26,000 multicolored, 7½-watt bulbs on five miles of electrical wire decorate the tree. There are no other ornaments except the lone five-foot star on top, which radiates a warm, white glow. The tree is usually a Norway Spruce with the height averaging between 65 and 75 feet tall. The largest tree measured 90 feet tall by 44 feet wide and weighed nine tons. Since 1954, Valerie Clarebout's 12 wire-sculpted herald angels have stood guard near the tree.

Biltmore Estate

A Gilded Age Christmas awaits visitors to America's largest home, the exquisite Biltmore Estate in Asheville, North Carolina. The home was built by George Vanderbilt and opened the night before Christmas in 1895. One of the enduring traditions begun by the Vanderbilts was to gather the staff and their children around the great 40-foot Fraser Fir in the Banquet Hall (pictured here) for a Christmas party and to give the children a holiday gift—and this charming tradition continues to this day. During the holidays, the estate is decked out with hundreds of fresh wreaths and poinsettias, thousands of

feet of evergreen roping, and more than 35 decorated trees. While visiting the estate, guests are entertained with Christmas choirs and musical ensembles. In 1998 a turn-of-the-century Saint Nicholas reads from Clement Moore's famous holiday tale, *A Visit From St. Nicholas.*

Christopher Radko

Collected by the likes of Elton John, Elizabeth Taylor, Whoopi Goldberg, and Barbra Streisand, the Christmas ornaments designed by Christopher Radko are some of the most extraordinary in the world. Radko developed his craft by accident—almost literally. In 1983 he was decorating his family's tree

with their treasure trove of 2,000 mouth-blown European glass ornaments when the tree stand gave way, toppling the tree and shattering over half the collection. "With sudden and resounding finality, it seemed that our door to the memories of Christmases past had slammed shut. We were devastated," Christopher recalls. When he searched to replace the broken handmade ornaments, he was disheartened to learn that they were almost impossible to find, both in the United States and Europe. Thus an industry was born. The designer has over 3,000 accounts that buy his spectacular creations, and he employs over 1,000 workers in Poland, Germany, Italy, and the Czech Republic, who painstakingly create the ornaments, each one taking seven days to complete. Radko has also used his success to benefit others and illuminate the true spirit of Christmas by donating over $1,000,000 to more than 20 charitable organizations.

Christopher Radko and Saks Fifth Avenue teamed up to present this luxurious 12-foot tree for an auction to benefit the Pediatric AIDS Foundation. Decorated with 1,000 glass ornaments and 5,000 lights, it brought a bid of $50,000.

Absolut
*W*orld renowned for innovative advertising campaigns, the Absolut Company adapts the Christmas tree into the shape of their trademark bottle.

Betsey Johnson

Her sense of style stands out in creative, cutting-edge fashions, and Betsey Johnson's Christmas tree is dressed in a style that is every bit as whimsical as the clothes she designs. With psychedelic gloves reaching out of the tree limbs and a punk *grrrl* angel straddling the top of the tree, this is every hipster's fantasy come true.

The Metropolitan Museum of Art

Since 1965, the Christmas tree at The Metropolitan Museum of Art in New York City, decorated with angels, cherubs, and the Christmas crèche, has been a favorite holiday attraction. Given to the museum by Loretta Hines Howard, the distinguished figures were originally from some of the great Neapolitan family cribs of the 18th century.

Harold Lloyd

Silent screen actor Harold Lloyd poses in front of his legendary Christmas tree in his Green Acres mansion. Mrs. Lloyd's love of Christmas was the inspiration for this great tree. Each year, friends, politicians, and movie stars sent the Lloyds Christmas ornaments from their travels. The famous Christmas tree, with its 5,000 decorations, completely dominated the Garden Room. First set up in 1965, the tree was made up of a combination of three fireproofed trees reaching sizes of 14 feet high, 9 feet wide, and almost 30 feet in circumference. The ornaments were valued from $5 to $150 in their day and many were one of a kind. There was an elaborately decorated ostrich egg, a sequined football, even a Christmas ball showing a miniature diorama of Harold Lloyd decorating his tree. Because the tree was so intricately designed, and Lloyd's charity work with numerous hospitals kept him so busy during the

holiday season, time did not permit putting it up and down each year, so it was kept up year round for many to enjoy. Mr. and Mrs. Lloyd's last tree stayed up for almost eight years.

American Museum of
Natural History

OrigamiUSA is a cultural arts organization headquartered in New York City's American Museum of Natural History. Each year the volunteers of OrigamiUSA spend thousands of hours decorating the tree, which is laden with colorful figures of dinosaurs, birds, plants, and animals. The tree is gloriously haloed by stars that represent the museum's Hayden Planetarium.

New York City Ballet

Taken from the classic E.T.A. Hoffman tale, *George Balanchine's The Nutcracker* is, according to Balanchine himself, "a serious thing wrapped in a fairy tale. *The Nutcracker*, at our theater, is a ballet about Christmas...for children and for adults who are children at heart. In every person the best, most important part is that which remains from his childhood." In Act One's "Party Scene" of New York City Ballet's production of *George Balanchine's The Nutcracker*, the Christmas tree is decorated in the German tradition, its boughs laden with food and toys, making it, symbolically, a tree of plenty.

Florence Griswold Museum

The home of America's best-known Impressionist art colony lies in the salt meadows and rocky upland pastures of Old Lyme, Connecticut. The guiding spirit of the art colony at Old Lyme was Miss Florence Griswold (1850–1937). Miss Florence was "big sister, soulmate, and mother superior" to an unruly group of American Impressionists who flocked to her boarding house from New York each summer to paint the special light that shimmered over the land along the Connecticut River and the Long Island Sound.

Christmas has always been a special time at the Florence Griswold Museum because Miss Griswold was born on Christmas Day in the same house that is now the museum.

The Florence Griswold Museum's dining room is lined on all sides with painted panels that were left in the house by the Lyme Art Colony artists as a gift to Miss Florence. The tree is decorated with strands of popcorn and cranberries and has charming cut-out cookies as ornaments.

Looking into the parlor of the Florence Griswold Museum. The painting over the mantle is by William Verplanck Birney. The tree is decorated with celestial angels, bruised plum and sage colored tassels, and vibrant pomegranate-hued ribbon.

27

Jane Seymour

$\mathcal{W}$hether in film or television, Jane Seymour conveys the elegance and style of a leading lady. Her exquisite, one-of-a-kind haute couture ball-gown tree is a magical fantasy woven of glittering gold, scarlet red, and pink satin, adorning a regal mannequin.

Dr. Christmas

Hollywood's "tree stylist to the stars," Dr. Christmas designs Christmas trees for some of the world's most celebrated names. Some of his favorite designs are tributes to Hollywood legends, including Sophia Loren, Bette Davis, Judy Garland, Lucille Ball, and Madonna (shown here).

Shirley MacLaine

Red and gold roses accent Shirley MacLaine's spectacular tree, combined with wintry frosted white and shining silver balls.

Melissa Gilbert
&
Bruce Boxleitner

Floral ribbons and a gold mesh garland make Melissa Gilbert and Bruce Boxleitner's tree a classic.

Barbara Eden

Blossoms of lilac- and sage-colored roses are artfully arranged on Barbara Eden's Christmas tree, along with miniature lavender rose garlands woven between bold violet ribbons. A dream to behold!

Bette Midler

$\mathcal{B}$ette Midler's
flocked tabletop tree was inspired by the
sea. It may be small in stature, but it is definitely
big in concept, using conch shells, golden
starfish, a grinning Midler mermaid, and a pink
plastic flamingo as decorations.

Newport Mansions

The 11 Newport Mansions in Newport, Rhode Island, harken back to an age of ease and splendor enjoyed by some of America's wealthiest families. Appropriately dubbed "America's First Castles," the Newport Mansions offer an exciting journey through more than 250 years of social and architectural history. Sprawling atop the cliffs of the Atlantic Ocean and beyond to the Narragansett Bay, these National Historic Landmark homes were once the summer "cottages" of the ultra-wealthy. Christmas at the mansions is mesmerizing, as many of the lovely estates are resplendent with trees authentically decorated to reflect their period in history.

The Breakers, built in 1895, was Cornelius Vanderbilt II's summer home. Nestled beneath this magnificent tree, there is a vintage train set representing the Vanderbilt family fortune, which was built on steamships and railroads.

The Elms mansion, built in 1901, is the setting for a "Belle Epoque" Christmas. Decorated for "Fete de Noel," a celebration of the French holiday traditions, the magnificent rooms are adorned with flowers and ribbons.

The Marble House's Gold Ballroom is the setting for this spectacular poinsettia tree. The house was built in 1892 for the William K. Vanderbilt family.

The Broadmoor

Named the "Grand Dame of the Rockies," the luxurious five-star, five-diamond Broadmoor hotel celebrates 80 years as the jewel resort of Colorado Springs, Colorado. Christmas at The Broadmoor is always a special time as the 3,000-acre property transforms into a magical wonderland of twinkling lights and snow-covered walkways. Over 300,000 lights adorn the hundred-plus conifers surrounding the spectacular resort, creating a dazzling forest of radiant Christmas trees greeting guests at every passageway.

Paul Newman

*L*egendary film star Paul Newman has a penchant for racing; he has even set a track record on the Grand Prix circuit. His sculpted racetrack tree sparkles with shining star flagpoles that line the route of a glittering gold and silver speedway.

Johnny Mathis

A statement in class, like the singer himself, Johnny Mathis' tree is certainly one of the best dressed, with white corsages, woven gold rope, elegant musical scrolls, and cascading ribbon.

Regal Biltmore Hotel

A National Historic Landmark hotel, the Regal Biltmore is located amidst the thriving business, financial, and cultural center of downtown Los Angeles. Opened with much fanfare in 1923, it has been home to presidents, kings, and Hollywood celebrities. The hotel is designed in the style of the Spanish-Italian Renaissance and is filled with exquisite frescoes and bas-relief decor. The elegant Christmas tree pictured in the hotel's lobby is tastefully decorated with ruby red bows, gold mesh garland, and turn-of-the-century ornaments. A sprightly cherub sits atop the tree surrounded by golden trumpets.

Henri Bendel

New York City boasts some of the world's finest shops, and it is no wonder that one of the premier stores in the city is Henri Bendel on 5th Avenue. Floral designer Robert Isabel created the Henri Bendel Holiday Spice Tree and Wreath, which has been a tradition at Henri Bendel since the early 1990s. The fragrant tree, shaped from baskets, and the Scandinavian-inspired wreath scent the air with the aroma of peppermint, cinnamon, allspice, nutmeg, and cardamom, treating shoppers to a feast for both the eyes and the nose.

Burt Reynolds

A burnished bronze star sits atop Burt Reynolds' topiary-themed tree. It is decorated with festive papier-mâché seasonal fruits—pears, apples, and cranberries—and tiny clay pots brimming with dried flowers.

Merv Griffin

Traditional country is the style of Merv Griffin's Christmas tree, with teddy bears made of straw, carved wooden toys, fragile dried flowers, bent wood wreaths, and gold-tipped pine cones.

Merv Griffin hosts an annual fundraising event at his Beverly Hilton Hotel called Christmas Tree Lane, where celebrities work with designers to decorate Christmas trees that are later auctioned off for charity. Some of the trees pictured in this book come from Christmas Tree Lane.

National Enquirer

Each year in tiny Lantana, Florida, the most incredible event occurred each Christmas season. Mr. Generoso Pope, the owner of the *National Enquirer*, would ship a Christmas tree unlike any other on display in the world to the grounds of the *Enquirer*'s 7.6-acre compound. Throughout the years, millions made the pilgrimage to see this vast conifer and enjoy the animated displays, the enormous model train exhibit, and the life-size manger scene. Standing in awe while the 15,200 twinkling lights sparkled high above their heads, people strained to get a glimpse of the glittering six-foot-high star beaming down on them. The 126-foot Douglas fir pictured here stood almost 13 stories high and weighed five tons, a symbol of great beauty and wonder. It has been 10 years since the last tree was erected in this magical place, but for those lucky souls who saw it, it remains a sight too extraordinary to forget.

Connie Stevens

All-out glitz and glamour went into the design of Connie Stevens' tree. It dazzles with glittering balls of fuschia, amethyst, and cobalt blue mixed with fantastic golden snowflakes.

Oscar de la Hoya

Boxing great Oscar de la Hoya demonstrates powerful attitude in his knock-out tree.

Lincoln Center

*T*he enormous tree in the front plaza of New York's Lincoln Center is breathtaking, with red, gold, and green twinkling lights, large golden musical instruments hung as ornaments, and a grand glowing snowflake perched on the top of the tree.

Tommy Tune

Elegant black top hats and sturdy wooden canes are every tap man's favorite props, and that is just what Tommy Tune envisioned for his stately Christmas tree.

Liza Minnelli

P

Propped atop a set of dancing legs is Liza Minnelli's merry Christmas tree that applauds the life of a showwoman, with silk stockings, glittering top hats, and a signature tie.

Leonard Bernstein

Golden trumpets, strands of gold beads, and exquisite purple and white satin bows make pianist Leonard Bernstein's Christmas tree a symphony of good taste.

Michael Bolton

Burnished-bronze musical notes and satin-printed melodic bows inspire Michael Bolton's exceptional tree.

The Beverly Hills Hotel

Since the early 20th century, The Beverly Hills Hotel has been the spot for Hollywood legends to socialize by the pool or romance the night away in cozy private bungalows, while studio moguls and Wall Street financiers consummate deals in the Polo Lounge. Holiday season at the hotel is the perfect time to

revel in the magic of tinseltown as lavish premiere parties, elegant soirées for two or two hundred, and festive poolside rendezvous are in full swing. The hotel brings all the charm of a traditional Christmas inside its glorious pink walls with its elaborate seasonal decor and host of merry carolers greeting guests upon their arrival in the hotel lobby.

Crystal Tree

Valued at half a million dollars, the Crystal Tree is certainly not for everyone! The tree is on display during the holiday season in a posh West Los Angeles crystal lighting store. A similar effect can be achieved with ropes of cut glass and gold wire for a mere one or two thousand dollars, but what fun is that?

Robin Leach

Robin Leach decorates his tree to reflect "the good life," surrounding it with a bottle of fine champagne on ice and trimming the worldly tree with Lear jets, shopping bags from Beverly Hills' exclusive Giorgio boutique, and strands of red ribbons from KRUG champagne.

Yoko Ono

Origami reindeer, Chinese masks and fans, and vibrantly colored figurines make Yoko Ono's tree an Asian celebration.

Anna Maria Tornaghi

Anna Maria Tornaghi's Brazilian-themed Christmas tree is a kaleidoscope of color, with brightly plumed macaws watching over their straw nests surrounded by a fiesta of tropical fruits and party balloons.

Keith Haring

Keith Haring's Christmas tree is hung with vivid canvases of turtledoves, geese, drummers, and more to form a striking palette that portrays *The Twelve Days of Christmas.*

Sharon Stone

L ike the popular film star's own personal
style, Sharon Stone's instinct for designing her
Christmas tree is refined and basic with no frills
attached. Decorated with lustrous red hearts and
twinkling amber lights, it is an expression of
understated subtlety.

Henry Ford Museum
&
Greenfield Village

Henry Ford Museum & Greenfield Village, located in Dearborn, Michigan, provides visitors with a unique educational experience based on authentic objects, stories, and lives representing America's traditions of ingenuity, resourcefulness, and innovation. The holiday season is breathtaking, as visitors to the Henry Ford Museum are greeted by a three-story Christmas tree inside the Great Hall. At least 2,000 ornaments decorate the tree and relate to items found in the museum's collection, such as automobiles, trains, airplanes, furniture, dishes and silverware, clocks, children's books, and teddy bears. More than 500 feet of real popcorn grace the stately tree as a garland. Air-popped with no salt, oil, or butter, the popcorn is strung on dental floss in 10- to 15-foot lengths, with a Velcro tab at each end to connect them.

Graceland

One of Elvis Presley's favorite places to be during the holidays was his home, Graceland, in Memphis, Tennessee. The Christmas decorations would go up just after Thanksgiving and remain in place at least through January 8, Elvis' birthday. A gaily decorated Christmas tree would be placed in the dining room, and the drapes would change to red to complement the table setting and offset the tree.

Opryland USA

When you step inside the Opryland Hotel, you enter a whole new world. It is a place where you experience all the charm and elegance of the South, and it is never more evident than in the days preceding Christmas. For the past 15 years the hotel has presented a "Country Christmas" celebration, one of the premier holiday events in the nation, including costumed carolers and a full-scale musical production. In mid-summer, crews begin stringing 2.2 million lights outside the hotel while indoors, under the enormous glass domes, the three interior gardens—the Conservatory, the Cascades, and the Delta—are festively attired.

More than two million lights illuminate the entrance to the Opryland Hotel.

The Delta garden room is especially colorful, with fabric garlands in gold, purple, fuchsia, and green adorning the massive Christmas tree.

Cactus Tree

*D*esert dwellers will find this cactus "Christmas tree" an alternative—albeit thorny—solution for their holiday decorating needs.

Roy Rogers & Dale Evans

*I*nspired by their love of the Old West, Roy Rogers and Dale Evans fashioned their Christmas tree out of horseshoes, wagon trains, lassos, and hundreds of cowboy collectibles.

Tumbleweed Tree

It is obvious that people will create their own special version of Christmas wherever they may find it. In this case, it is a towering tumbleweed Christmas tree—photographed in Arizona in 1974—adorned with lights and a golden star.

Vincent Price

A sense of the macabre enlivens Vincent Price's haunted Christmas tree. Hung with skeletons, cobwebs, and slimy worms, this tree is not for the faint of spirit.

Pioneer Square

Since 1984, a towering Christmas tree, generously donated to the city of Portland, Oregon, by a local timber company, has been erected in Pioneer Courthouse Square. The Friends of Pioneer Courthouse Square started this lovely tradition as part of a beautification project, taking what was once an abandoned parking lot and transforming it into a gorgeous public space. This same site was also significant for being the location of Portland's first school. Every year, a Grand Fir weighing up to 10,000 pounds and reaching between 75 and 95 feet in height is trucked in, and the tree is lit the Friday following Thanksgiving with much pageantry and fanfare, attracting crowds of 20,000 onlookers. The 7,000 twinkling lights, streaming red sashes, and the golden star on top, measuring four-and-a-half feet in diameter, illuminate this special place—a tribute to the generous people of Portland, Oregon.

The Jackson Tower Building keeps watch over the Christmas tree at Pioneer Courthouse Square.

Hearst Castle

Magnificent Hearst Castle in San Simeon, California, is the former home of newspaper publisher William Randolph Hearst and is now a State Historical Monument. The castle is filled with Christmas decorations during the month of December, reminiscent of its heyday, the 1930s. Garlands and wreaths adorn the doorways and fireplaces of Casa Grande, the main residence at Hearst Castle, and poinsettias and baskets of greenery fill the rooms. The Christmas tree pictured here is from the Assembly Room, and there are actually two trees in this massive 82 x 30-foot chamber, one at each end, surrounded by brightly wrapped gifts and toys.

Hotel del Coronado

A Victorian masterpiece resort and National Historic Landmark, the Hotel del Coronado is situated along 26 lush oceanfront acres on the Pacific Ocean in the quaint seaside village of Coronado. Located across the bay from San Diego, California, it has been celebrating the holidays in the grand tradition since 1888. One of America's first electrically lighted outdoor Christmas trees was on view at The Del in 1904, setting the stage for a century of holiday enchantment. Each year, a 30-foot Noble Fir is decorated with a different holiday theme and is bedecked with thousands of sparkling white lights. Many families flock to the hotel at Christmastime to visit the beautiful tree and share a yuletide dinner in the magnificent Crown Room. Host to presidents, dignitaries, Hollywood celebrities, and travelers from around the world, the Hotel del Coronado is a treasured Southern California resort.

The White House

Based on daughter Chelsea's love of the ballet, President and Mrs. Clinton had the 18'6" Colorado Blue Spruce tree in the White House designed to encompass all the elements from *The Nutcracker* ballet. The decorations on the tree come from three distinct and talented groups: Regional and professional ballet companies contributed ornaments that represented their own performances of *The Nutcracker*, wood craft artisans created ornaments depicting scenes or characters from the ballet, and members of the American Needlepoint Guild and the Embroiderers Guild of America stitched holiday stockings to hang on the tree. The green velvet handmade tree skirt was designed by individuals from each of the 50 states, U.S. territories, and the District of Columbia, in celebration of the Clinton family's Christmas holiday at the White House in 1996.

The elegant East Room displays the traditional White House crèche made in Naples, Italy, in the late 18th century. It contains 47 carved wood and terra-cotta figures and is flanked by two stately trees decorated in bronze, claret, and gold.

Julia Roberts

Golden bows, violet ribbons, and an elegant fleur-de-lis with a splash of tulle make Julia Roberts' tree as pretty and vivacious as the star herself.

Rosie
O'Donnell

Garlands of silk flowers, pink ribbons, and whispy angels adorn Rosie O'Donnell's childlike and strikingly feminine Christmas tree.

The Breakers

Patterned after the Villa Medici in Rome, The Breakers in Palm Beach, Florida, is an Italian Renaissance–style hotel founded in 1896 and set amid lush, tropical greenery and pristine white sand beaches. It is listed on the National Register of Historic Places and is both a Mobil Five-Star and an AAA five-diamond resort. The tastefully decorated Christmas tree is adorned to reflect an Old World Mediterranean flavor. It resides gracefully on a stone column in the main lobby amidst hand-painted decorative vaulted ceilings for all to admire.

Pia Zadora

The Big Apple is the theme of Pia Zadora's New York City Christmas tree. Taxi cabs, the theatre, shopping sprees, and the trademark bagel make her tree simply *mah-vel-ous*.

David
Hasselhoff

As the quintessential California beach dude, David Hasselhoff can bring out the surfer in everyone. His tree is decorated with suntan lotion, flip flops, lifeguard boats, California license plates, and, of course, a suntanned Ken® doll!

Fashion Island

*F*ashion Island shopping center is located in beautiful Newport Beach, California, and is one of Southern California's preeminent shopping and dining destinations. Swaying palm trees and ocean views are not the backdrop you would imagine for the location of the country's (and possibly the world's) tallest Christmas tree, but that is exactly where you will find this 110-foot White Fir. It takes a staff of five people approximately three days, practically working around the clock, to bedeck this towering tannenbaum with its 10,000 white lights and 8,000 elegant red and gold ornaments.

Knott's Berry Farm

Since the 1930s, families have delighted in visiting Southern California's "hometown" theme park, the venerable Knott's Berry Farm. Christmas becomes an especially jubilant occasion, as the park transforms into Knott's Merry Farm®, with lavish decorations and live yuletide shows. An enchanting Victorian shopping village rises out of the ashes of Ghost Town, with dozens of artisans selling one-of-a-kind seasonal crafts. The biggest treat, though, is seeing the Peanuts characters, in their winter finery, cheerfully greeting people in front of the enormous Christmas tree decorated with sparking lights, jewel-colored glass balls, and trademark boysenberry ornaments.

Marshall Field's

*C*hicago's Marshall Field's is one of the premier department stores in the United States and certainly one of the oldest, opening in 1852. As early as the 1920s, Marshall Field's was displaying live evergreen Christmas trees in the famous Walnut Room (the first dining room/restaurant in any department store) in the flagship State Street store. Called "The Great Tree of Marshall Field's," it stands 45 feet tall and contains over 1,200 handcrafted ornaments and 15,000 lights. Every year the tree is redecorated, and families come from hundreds of miles away to watch the official tree-lighting ceremony, followed by a robust holiday lunch.

Toys for Tots

A portion of the proceeds from the sale of this book will go directly to Toys for Tots, a U.S. Marine Corps Reserve Program. In 1947, Major Bill Hendricks, USMCR—with the help of his Los Angeles Marine Corps Reserve Unit—collected and distributed 5,000 toys to needy children. Bill's program was so successful that in 1948, the Marine Corps adopted it and expanded it nationwide. For Christmas 1997, the 50th anniversary of the U.S. Marine Corps Reserve Toys for Tots Program, Marines distributed over 10,000,000 toys to more than 4,700,000 needy children nationwide via local social welfare agencies and churches.

How you can help

Donate a toy to your local USMC Reserve Unit

Donate your time to help local Marines

Donate service support to local Marines
- Collection receptacles at your business
- Warehouse space
- Transportation support
- Media exposure

Make a tax-deductible donation to: Marine Toys for Tots Foundation, P.O. Box 1947, Quantico, VA 22134

Acknowledgments

With special thanks to Kurt Wahlner and Trici Venola, whose visionary Christmas tree was the inspiration for this book; Quay Hays, for his encouragement; my mother, Lelah Jackson, who suggested some of the trees found herein and who created the special magic of Christmas for myself and my three brothers every year in our home; Lisa Delena for her sojourn to Victorville; Sheri Parris for her quest for all things purple; Mon Muellerschoen for describing Christmas traditions in Germany; the GPG staff for humoring me, my editor, Dana Stibor, and my publicist, Mina Silverstone; the numerous talented florists and designers who helped create the celebrity trees; Paula Sautter at the Beverly Hilton Hotel; Suzanne Lloyd Hayes, granddaughter and trustee for the Harold Lloyd Estate; C.L. Arbelbide for sharing her knowledge of national holiday traditions; Kitty Hall at Absolut; Lisa Marriott at the Beverly Hills Hotel; Jane Cox and Kelly Hoisington at Biltmore Estate; Kyle Hall at Christopher Radko/STARAD; Bob Pranga for Dr. Christmas; Nina Robinson at Fashion Island; Steve Miller at New York City Ballet; John Alba at the German Information Center; Todd Anderson at Graceland; Jim Allen and DeRoy Jensen at Hearst Castle; Lauren Ash Donoho at Hotel del Coronado; Mathew Schliesman and Bob Ochnser at Knott's Berry Farm; Julie Kasper at the American Museum of Natural History; Andrea Schwartz at Marshall Field's; Deanna Cross at the Metropolitan Museum of Art; G. Todd Smith at Opryland USA; Sheena Stevens at the Regal Biltmore Hotel; Jennifer Genco at The Breakers; Kristin Koca-Miller at The Broadmoor; Jack Becker at The Florence Griswold Museum; Tina Benvenuti at The Henry Ford Museum; Suzanne Larson at The Preservation Society of Newport County; William Allman at the White House; Nora Kean at Tishman Spear Properties for Rockefeller Center; Joan Cannata-Fox at National Enquirer; Teril Lindquist-Turner at Henri Bendel, and, especially, Major William J. Grein and Lieutenant Matthew T. Cooper at the Marine Toys for Tots Foundation.

Index/Photo Credits

Absolut, 16, photo courtesy of The Absolut Company

American Museum of Natural History, 22–23, photo by Adam Anik, courtesy of the Department of Library Services, American Museum of Natural History

Leonard Bernstein, 54, © Globe Photos, Inc.

The Beverly Hills Hotel, 56–57, photos courtesy of The Beverly Hills Hotel

Biltmore Estate, 12–13, photos courtesy of Biltmore Estate, Asheville, North Carolina

Michael Bolton, 55, © Celebrity Photo Agency

The Breakers, 84–85, photos courtesy of The Breakers

The Broadmoor, 36–37, photos courtesy of The Broadmoor

Cactus Tree, 70, © Index Stock Photography

Crystal Tree, 58, © Globe Photos, Inc.

Oscar de la Hoya, 49, © Celebrity Photo Agency

Dr. Christmas, 29, © Bob Pranga

Barbara Eden, 32, © Celebrity Photo Agency

Fashion Island, 88, photos courtesy of Fashion Island, Newport Beach

Florence Griswold Museum, 26–27, photos courtesy of the Lyme Historical Society

Melissa Gilbert and Bruce Boxleitner, 31, © Celebrity Photo Agency

Graceland, 66–67, © Elvis Presley Enterprises, Inc.

Merv Griffin, 45, © Celebrity Photo Agency

Keith Haring, 62, © Globe Photos, Inc.

David Hasselhoff, 87, © Celebrity Photo Agency

Hearst Castle, 76–77, photos courtesy of Hearst Castle™/Hearst San Simeon State Historical Monument™

Henri Bendel, 42–43, photos courtesy of Henri Bendel

Henry Ford Museum & Greenfield Village, 64, photo courtesy of the Henry Ford Museum & Greenfield Village, Dearborn, Michigan

Hotel del Coronado, 78: © Carol Peerce, 79: photo courtesy of the Hotel del Coronado

Betsey Johnson, 17, © Globe Photos, Inc.

Knott's Berry Farm, 89, photo courtesy of Knott's Berry Farm

Robin Leach, 59, © Globe Photos, Inc.

Lincoln Center, 50–51, © Globe Photos, Inc.

Harold Lloyd, 20–21, © Globe Photos, Inc.

Shirley MacLaine, 30, © Celebrity Photo Agency

Marshall Field's, 90–91, photos courtesy of Marshall Field's

Johnny Mathis, 39, © Celebrity Photo Agency

The Metropolitan Museum of Art, 18–19, The Metropolitan Museum of Art, Gift of Loretta Hines Howard, 1964 (64.164.1-167), © 1995 The Metropolitan Museum of Art

Bette Midler, 33, © Globe Photos, Inc.

Liza Minnelli, 53, © Globe Photos, Inc.

National Enquirer, 46–47, photo courtesy of the *National Enquirer*

Paul Newman, 38, © Celebrity Photo Agency

Newport Mansions, 34–35, photos property of The Preservation Society of Newport County

New York City Ballet, 24–25, *George Balanchine's The Nutcracker* © The George Balanchine Trust, photo by Paul Kolnik, scenery by Rouben Ter-Arutunian, costumes by Karinska

Rosie O'Donnell, 83, © Celebrity Photo Agency

Yoko Ono, 60, © Globe Photos, Inc.

Opryland USA, 68–69, © Donnie Beauchamp

Pioneer Square, 74–75, photo by Larry Geddis Photography

Vincent Price, 73, © Globe Photos, Inc.

Christopher Radko, 14–15, photos courtesy of Christopher Radko

Regal Biltmore Hotel, 40–41, photos courtesy the Regal Biltmore Hotel

Burt Reynolds, 44, © Celebrity Photo Agency

Julia Roberts, 82, © Celebrity Photo Agency

Rockefeller Center, 10–11, © Bart Barlow, courtesy of Rockefeller Center, Tishman Speyer Properties

Roy Rogers & Dale Evans, 71, photo by Lisa Delena

Jane Seymour, 28, © Celebrity Photo Agency

Connie Stevens, 48, © Celebrity Photo Agency

Sharon Stone, 63, © Celebrity Photo Agency

Anna Maria Tornaghi, 61, © Globe Photos, Inc.

Toys for Tots, 92, photo courtesy of Marines Toys for Tots Foundation

Tumbleweed Tree, 72, © Globe Photos, Inc.

Tommy Tune, 52, © Globe Photos, Inc.

White House, 80–81, © Globe Photos, Inc.

Pia Zadora, 86, © Globe Photos, Inc.

Other Photo Credits:

4: Tony Stone Images/Josh Mitchell
6: Courtesy of German Information Center
7: Courtesy of German Information Center
8 (left): Courtesy of German Information Center
8 (right): Corbis
9: Corbis
93: AP/Wide World Photos